The Six Wives of Henry VIII

'Divorced, beheaded, died; divorced, beheaded, survived'

– the rhyme tells the fate of Henry VIII's six wives. Henry was passionately in love with all but one
of his wives, but it wasn't love that drove him to marry so many times. It was his desperate desire
to provide a male heir for the throne of England, for in Tudor times it was generally
agreed that only a male could provide strong government.

Even in Tudor times, however, Henry's behaviour appalled the courts of Europe and we can only
marvel at the courage of Catherine Parr, his sixth wife, in agreeing to marry the obese, evil-tempered,
ulcerous old man. This hideous picture of Henry is in sharp contrast to the young king, who was
described in 1519 by a Venetian ambassador as 'The handsomest monarch I ever set eyes upon:
above the usual height ... with a round face so very beautiful it would become a pretty woman.'
It was with this man that Henry's first wife, Catherine of Aragon, fell in love.

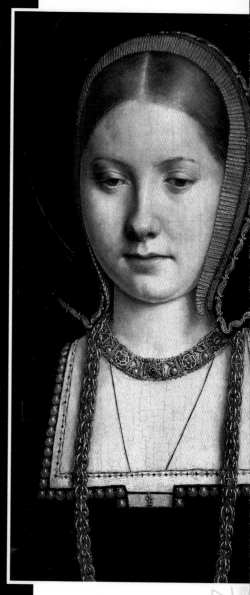

CATHERINE FIRST MET HENRY when he was ten and she was 16. She had come to England to marry his older brother Arthur and, after a three-month journey from Spain and with Henry riding beside her, this gentle, pious girl was welcomed into London by cheering crowds. Catherine had always known that one day she would be queen of England. Her marriage to Prince Arthur, the heir to the English throne, had been arranged when Catherine was just three years old, to cement an alliance between England and the powerful nation of Spain.

After their wedding, Catherine and Arthur took up residence in Ludlow Castle on the Welsh border, but within six months the 15-year-old Arthur had died. Little is known about those few months in Ludlow, but Catherine later claimed that the marriage was unconsummated. Nevertheless for a new marriage to be arranged between Catherine and her brother-in-law, Prince Henry, a special dispensation was first required from the Pope. Since Henry was not yet 12 years old, the wedding had to wait until he was 14 and could give his consent.

By then, Henry VII no longer needed the alliance with Spain and advised his son to repudiate the betrothal. Prince Henry did so, claiming it had been arranged without his consent, but four years later, when his father died and Henry became king, he immediately married Catherine. He may have done this to assert his independence, but it is just as likely that he was attracted to Catherine herself. She was intelligent, accomplished and politically astute, having acted as an ambassador for Spain for several years. Henry and Catherine brought vitality and *joie de vivre* to court life, with sumptuous banquets, tournaments and entertainments.

Catherine was well aware that her role as queen was to bear children. In 1511 Henry and Catherine were delighted by the birth of a son, Prince Henry, but sadly he lived for only a few weeks. Catherine was soon pregnant again, yet of her next five pregnancies, only one produced a living child, Princess Mary, in 1516.

CATHERINE OF ARAGON'S BADGE

Catherine's badge shows a pomegranate with a crown above it.

YOUNG CATHERINE

Catherine was the youngest daughter of Ferdinand of Aragon and Isabella of Castile, the rulers of Spain. She came to England in 1501 to marry Prince Arthur and after his death remained in England for seven uncertain years until her marriage to Henry VIII in 1509.

HENRY AND CATHERINE'S CORONATION

A contemporary woodcut shows the coronation of Henry VIII and Catherine on 24 June 1509. The Tudor rose symbolizes Henry and the pomegranate identifies Catherine. There is little doubt that in the early years of their marriage, the couple were in love.

LUDLOW CASTLE

Catherine and Arthur lived in this castle, isolated on the Welsh borders, during the winter of 1501/02. Catherine had her own Spanish household, but neither Catherine nor Arthur would have been able to speak Welsh.

PRINCE ARTHUR

Catherine's first husband was Henry's elder brother, Arthur, shown here on a design for a stained-glass window. Never very strong, Arthur died of what was called consumption, but was probably pneumonia, on 2 April 1502. He was buried in Worcester Cathedral.

ROYAL PSALTER

Both Elizabeth of York (Henry's mother) and Catherine of Aragon owned a 14th-century psalter made by Humphrey de Bohun. Their signatures are shown on the fly-leaf with the words 'Thys Booke ys myn'.

The King's 'Great Matter'

FOLLOWING THE BIRTH OF PRINCESS MARY in 1516, Henry put on a brave face. 'The queen and I are both young and if it is a girl this time, by God's grace boys will follow,' he declared. Another miscarriage followed instead, in 1518, and Henry's affections began to wander.

In 1519 his mistress, Elizabeth Blount, gave birth to a son, Henry Fitzroy, whom Henry VIII, increasingly desperate about the lack of a male heir, acknowledged. Henry Fitzroy was made Duke of Richmond in 1525, in preparation perhaps to naming him heir. But by 1525 a new face – that of Anne Boleyn – had appeared at the English court and caught Henry's attention.

Catherine was clearly too old to have any more children and Henry became convinced that God was punishing him. He quoted the text from Leviticus: 'If a man shall take his brother's wife it is an unclean thing … they shall be childless.' The Pope's earlier dispensation, Henry claimed, was invalid. Catherine, however, believed deeply in the sanctity and validity of her marriage. Henry wanted Catherine to enter a nunnery and so annul the marriage, but she refused. In 1532 the queen was publicly isolated and separated from her daughter.

Cardinal Wolsey, Henry's powerful chief minister, was given the task of securing a divorce for Henry, but the Pope refused and Wolsey was dismissed. Thomas Cranmer and Thomas Cromwell advised a different solution: they encouraged Henry's belief that the Pope had no jurisdiction over him. In 1533 Cranmer was appointed Archbishop of Canterbury and almost at once links with Rome were severed and the marriage between Catherine and Henry annulled.

Catherine never accepted the new state of affairs. Even after Henry had married Anne Boleyn, Catherine considered herself the rightful queen. She lived the rest of her life in isolation and died in 1536. Although it is said that Henry rejoiced when he heard the news of her death, his marriage to Anne was already in difficulty.

BUCKDEN PALACE
After Henry left her for Anne Boleyn in 1528, Catherine lived here in Huntingdonshire with her diminished household. Catherine refused many of Henry's demands, but did reluctantly hand over the royal jewels to Anne Boleyn.

THE OLDER CATHERINE
This miniature of Catherine was painted about the time Henry fell in love with Anne Boleyn. Repeated pregnancies and miscarriages had taken their toll on her looks, her spirits and her health. She became ever more pious, even wearing a rough Franciscan habit under her royal robes.

FIRST ENGLISH BIBLE

This New Testament was printed and published by
William Tyndale in Antwerp in 1534. Tyndale was the
first person to translate the Bible into English and he was
declared a heretic by Sir Thomas More. Catherine of
Aragon's coat of arms is at the foot of the cover.

PRINCESS MARY

Princess Mary was separated from Catherine after
1532 but she was as obdurate as her mother. She
refused to acknowledge Catherine's successor and
caused much disruption in Anne's royal household.

CATHERINE ARGUES HER CASE

This painting by Sir John Gilbert shows
Henry and Catherine arguing in front of the
Cardinals. Both Wolsey and Campeggio
begged Catherine to agree to Henry's demands
for an annulment to the marriage. Catherine
refused, arguing right up to her death that
the marriage was valid.

Anne Boleyn

WHO WAS ANNE BOLEYN? She was not, like Catherine, a European princess, nor did she have royal ancestry. It is not known for certain when she was born, but it was probably in 1501. She was the niece of the Duke of Norfolk and daughter of Sir Thomas Boleyn, and, when she was 12 years old, she was sent to Brussels to become a maid of honour to the archduchess Margaret, Regent of the Netherlands. The Regent was pleased with her: 'I find her so bright and pleasant for her young age.'

Anne was neither beautiful nor pretty, but she did have a vivacious personality and the advantage of a European education at the sophisticated French court, where she was sent in 1514 to act as interpreter for Mary, Henry's sister. When Mary returned to England a widow, Anne stayed in France in the service of Queen Claude. She gained elegance and poise and grew interested in religious reform.

In 1522 Anne returned to England and entered the royal court. Here this tall, black-haired and dark-eyed young woman, with her quick wit and magnetic appeal, was much sought after in the flirtatious games played by the nobility. In 1526 she caught the king's eye. Henry fell in love with her, but Anne played a bold and skilful game. For six years, the couple met, hunted and danced together, but Anne refused to sleep with Henry unless he married her. Henry was just as anxious for marriage: he needed legitimate sons and he was now relying on Anne to provide them.

As Henry's difficulties with Catherine dragged on, Anne and Henry began to consort more openly and in 1532 they finally slept together. By December Anne was pregnant. They married secretly in January 1533 and the king eagerly prepared for the birth of a son.

ANNE BOLEYN'S BADGE
Anne Boleyn's badge shows a crowned falcon with Tudor rose; her motto was 'Most happy'.

ANNE BOLEYN

This drawing of Anne Boleyn is by Holbein. A Venetian diarist who saw Anne at Calais in 1532 described her as 'not one of the handsomest women in the world; ... swarthy complexion, long neck, wide mouth ... eyes which are black and beautiful'.

JEWEL CASE

This 16th-century jewel casket is thought to have belonged to Anne Boleyn.

COURTSHIP

This Victorian painting by William Powell Frith shows Henry and Anne shooting in Windsor Forest. Henry was passionately in love with Anne and struggled for many years to get a divorce from Catherine in order to marry her.

HEVER CASTLE

Anne probably spent her early years here at Hever Castle, the family seat, in Kent. Hever Castle was later given to Anne of Cleves, who spent many of the last years of her life here.

HENRY ARRIVES AT HEVER

During their long courtship, Henry often visited Anne at Hever and they would stroll together in the grounds.

Anne's Downfall

IN SEPTEMBER 1533 Princess Elizabeth was born. The celebrations went ahead, but Henry's bitter disappointment affected their already stormy relationship, which alternated between furious quarrels and passionate reconciliations. Anne knew that to secure her position she must produce a son, but in July 1534 she miscarried.

By the time Catherine died in January 1536, Anne was pregnant again. This pregnancy too, however, was doomed. At the end of January, she miscarried again and this time she lost a son. Henry felt that his second marriage was following the pattern of the first: God must still be angry with him. He lamented his bad fortune, but he did not blame Anne – yet. Just three months later, it was a different story.

Anne had never been popular with the people, as Catherine had, and her position as queen was resented by many at court. She was blamed for Henry's brutalities, such as the executions of Bishop John Fisher and Sir Thomas More. In April 1536, Anne's enemies combined to bring about her downfall. They told the king that she had committed adultery and plotted treason against him. They even said that she had committed incest with her brother. Although the charges were clearly untrue, Henry's passion swung against her.

Anne was arrested on 2 May and taken to the Tower of London. Henry called her a 'cursed and poisoning whore' and claimed that she had bewitched and seduced him. She was tried in the Tower of London. In court she calmly and convincingly denied all the charges, but, although there was no proof, she was condemned. To humiliate her further, Henry used his own previous affair with her sister Mary as reason to have the marriage annulled. Two days later Anne was beheaded.

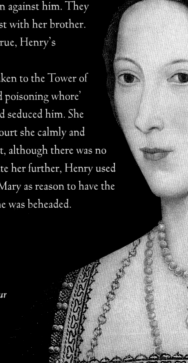

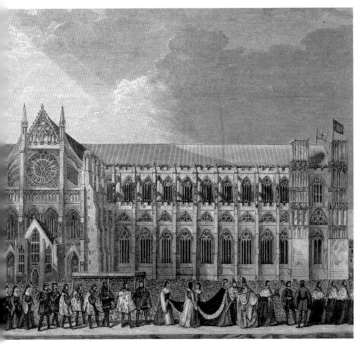

MUSIC FROM AN ADMIRER

This music book was compiled for Anne by Mark Smeaton, a musician of the King's Privy Chamber. The illustration in the middle of the page shows the falcon (Anne's symbol) pecking a pomegranate (Catherine's symbol). Smeaton was infatuated with Anne, but she rejected him. When Smeaton was tortured in 1536, he confessed to an affair with Anne and so condemned them both.

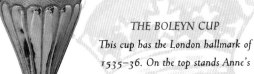

THE BOLEYN CUP

This cup has the London hallmark of 1535–36. On the top stands Anne's falcon. The cup was probably given as one of the queen's New Year's gifts.

THE TOWER OF LONDON

When Anne stayed here the night before her coronation, she little knew she would return just three years later to face trial for treason. Her final journey from Greenwich took two hours and by the time she arrived she was hysterical – weeping and laughing by turn. On 19 May 1536 she was executed here.

Jane Seymour

Henry was betrothed to Jane Seymour and just 10 days later they were married at Whitehall. Jane's place at court had been very similar to Anne's. She had no royal blood and was the fifth child of Sir John Seymour, a respected courtier. She had been lady in waiting to both her predecessors, but any similarity to Anne ended there. In personality she was the complete opposite.

Whereas Anne had been flirtatious, vivacious and coquettish, Jane was sweet-natured, sensible and docile. She was also pale-faced and rather stolid-looking. She was about 27 years old – rather old to be still unmarried in Tudor times – when Henry became interested in her. She was modest and virtuous: in the early months of 1536, after Anne's final miscarriage, Henry began to pursue Jane, but she rebuffed his advances, returning a present of money with the admonition that she would accept it only as a dowry when she married.

After their marriage she immediately tried to bring peace and calm to Henry's court and family. When Mary at last gave in and was reconciled with Henry, Jane welcomed her to court and became close friends with her. Henry was delighted with his new wife, particularly when she became pregnant.

In September 1537 she retired to Hampton Court to prepare for the birth. Her labour was long and difficult, taking two days and three nights, but on 12 October the longed-for son was born. Bonfires were lit across the nation, wine flowed and Henry is said to have wept for joy. Two thousand guns were fired from the Tower of London, but the joy was short-lived. On 18 October, Jane became ill with childbed fever, a common infection for which there was then no cure. On 24 October, Henry's 'entirely beloved' wife died. The king was grief-stricken and went into deep mourning for several months.

JANE SEYMOUR
A portrait by Holbein of Jane Seymour, a quiet and gentle person who nevertheless was adept at managing Henry. Unlike Anne Boleyn, Jane knew how far to press her advantages and when to stop.

JANE SEYMOUR'S BADGE
Jane Seymour's badge shows a phoenix atop a castle sprouting Tudor roses. Her motto was 'Bound to obey and serve'.

THE ROYAL NURSERY

This happy picture of Henry playing with the young Prince Edward in his nursery was painted by Marcus Stone (1840–1921). It shows how delighted Henry was with his son.

PRINCE EDWARD

Prince Edward as a boy, one of many portraits that the king commissioned of his son. Henry had waited 29 years for the birth of an heir and was 46 years old when Edward was born.

Henry not only treated four of his wives appallingly badly, he became increasingly tyrannical. What happened to the young prince of whom de Puebla wrote in 1507 'there is no finer youth in the world'? Did frustration and disappointment change him or was he born autocratic? He was certainly headstrong when young and, surrounded by adulation and flattery, he soon acquired a grandiose sense of his own superiority. Like most tyrants, Henry believed in the absolute validity of everything he did and, when things went wrong, he blamed someone else.

With the benefit of hindsight we can see that Henry's insistence on having a son was unjust and mistaken, but his view was supported by the wisdom of the time. England had recently been through a long period of civil war and both Henry and his father believed that a strong ruler was essential for stability. If a girl inherited the throne, power in England would pass to her husband and could lead to foreign domination.

Much of Henry's behaviour, however, was illogical and his desire for a son seems to have become an obsession. Henry greatly admired Jane Seymour's father, who had fathered four sons before Jane was born: the young Henry had even joked with Sir John Seymour about his celebrated virility. If sons were a sign of virility, where did that leave Henry? Believing that God was angry with him, he blamed his wives.

Why did Henry go to the unnecessary trouble of having his marriage to Anne annulled when she was about to be executed? Was it an act of revenge for wounded pride? Ironically, in claiming that the marriage had never been valid, he actually exonerated her from the charges of adulterous treason for which she was being beheaded. And by having the marriages to Catherine and Anne annulled, he made his only legitimate heirs illegitimate. He was determined to start afresh with his 'true wife', Jane.

There is a final irony: both of Henry's daughters became strong rulers, and Elizabeth became one of England's greatest monarchs.

HENRY AS A CHILD
This sketch of Henry as a young child shows the same wide mouth and eyes as the sculpture below. Henry was a robust, intelligent child who enjoyed riding, tennis and other physical activities.

...the Changing

HENRY AGED 45

This portrait was painted in the year he married Jane Seymour. Although he is splendidly dressed, he shows signs of increasing weight and age: his hat covers a bald head and his beard hides a disappearing chin. His mouth has become tight and his eyes inspire fear rather than admiration.

HENRY AGED NEARLY 50

By the time Henry married Catherine Howard he often referred to himself as an old man. He hoped his marriage to Catherine would rejuvenate him.

HENRY IN HIS FINAL YEARS

A 16th-century engraving shows Henry as a gross and bitter old man. People were so afraid of him, no one dared to tell him he was dying.

e of Henry VIII

THE 'RENAISSANCE PRINCE'

In 1519 the Venetian ambassador described Henry as '... extremely handsome; nature could not have done more for him ...'. He was unusually tall and very charming.

Anne of Cleves

THERE WAS NO DOUBT AFTER JANE DIED that Henry would marry again. The question was, who? Now that a prince had been born, there was less pressure to produce an heir, although a duke of York (a second son) would be much welcomed.

Royal marriage in Tudor times had another function: political alliance. Since Henry's break with Rome, England had been isolated from the two strongest European powers, France and Spain. If they combined against Henry, England would be in trouble. The principality of Cleves, however, was part of an up-and-coming Protestant state in Germany. The Duke of Cleves was allied to Saxony and the league of Lutheran princes, and he had two unmarried sisters.

Thomas Cromwell, the king's chief minister, was excited at the possibility of an alliance, but Henry was cautious. He wanted to know what the sisters looked like – were they beautiful? The two women had been so heavily clothed the envoys could not tell, so the painter Holbein travelled to Cleves to paint them. Henry was satisfied with the portrait of Anne and a marriage contract was drawn up.

Anne had a long and difficult journey to England. Henry was so impatient to see his new bride that he rode from Greenwich to Rochester to meet her. As soon as he saw her, on New Year's Day 1540, his heart sank. 'I like her not,' he told Cromwell. Apart from her lack of good looks, Anne spoke only German and was ill-equipped for life at the sophisticated English court. She neither played an instrument, sang nor read books: all she could do was sew.

Henry knew it was too late to stop the marriage and the wedding went ahead on 6 January, but, although he shared Anne's bed, he could not bring himself to consummate the marriage. It took only six months for a divorce to be arranged. Unlike Catherine of Aragon, Anne did not dispute the proceedings and quietly accepted the title of 'King's sister', along with various houses and lands.

ANNE OF CLEVES' BADGE
Anne's badge shows the coronet of the Duke of Cleves.

ANNE'S MARRIAGE SETTLEMENT

This document gave Anne £4,377 a year. When the marriage was annulled just
six months after the wedding, Henry gave Anne a generous settlement of manors
and estates, which included the palace of Richmond and Hever Castle.

RICHMOND

RICHMOND PALACE

Anne of Cleves was staying in
Richmond Palace when she
heard the news of her divorce
from Henry. It is said that
Anne was so innocent and
unsophisticated that she was
unaware her marriage had
not been consummated.

THOMAS CROMWELL

Thomas Cromwell was blamed
for the fiasco of the Anne of
Cleves marriage and for
everything else that was
going wrong for Henry. On
10 June 1540 he was
arrested and on 28 July he
was executed.

Catherine Howard

IF ANNE OF CLEVES WAS DULL and inexperienced, Catherine Howard certainly was not. She was one of the younger daughters of Lord Edmund Howard and was high-spirited and sexually precocious. She had her first love affair at the age of 15 and, between 1537 and 1539, she and Francis Dereham were lovers. In 1540, at the age of 19, she came to court as lady-in-waiting to the new queen, Anne of Cleves.

Henry noticed her almost at once and was greatly attracted to her. Although small and no great beauty, she was vivacious and fun-loving – a distinct contrast to Anne of Cleves, whom he could not abide. Just 19 days after his divorce from Anne, he married Catherine, on 28 July. Henry was wildly happy, full of energy and zest for his young wife. He showered her with lands, jewels and clothes. Catherine in turn showered her many relatives with jobs at court.

Henry was now overweight and ageing, and he had an ulcer on his leg which never healed. His good mood soon alternated with ill-temper and depression. In 1541 Catherine renewed her relationship with Thomas Culpepper, a former admirer, and appointed Francis Dereham, her former lover, as her secretary. By September rumours were circulating at court. Catherine's enemies seized their chance. In November the king was told about her early affairs, but Henry would not believe that his adored queen, his 'very jewel of womanhood', was anything but innocent and ordered an enquiry to prove it.

The enquiry, however, found proof that not only had she been unchaste when he married her, but that she was now flirting under his very nose. Henry had been cuckolded: his pride was shattered and he swore he would torture her to death himself. He wept with rage and self-pity. Culpepper and Dereham were executed on 10 December 1541.

In February 1542 Catherine was taken from Hampton Court to the Tower of London. Only then did she seem to grasp the full seriousness of her situation and wept constantly. On 13 February she was beheaded.

CATHERINE HOWARD

Born in 1521, Catherine was only 19 when Henry married her. Impressionable and ill educated, she was easily used by the Duke of Norfolk and other members of the Howard family to further their ambitions.

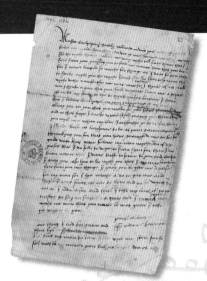

THOMAS CRANMER, ARCHBISHOP OF CANTERBURY

When Cranmer received information about Catherine's early
affairs, he felt he had to inform the king, thus
precipitating her downfall.

HAUNTED GALLERY

It is said that Catherine's ghost has been heard shrieking
in the Haunted Gallery at Hampton Court.

TRAITOR'S GATE

Catherine was brought in a sealed barge
through Traitor's Gate to the Tower of London.
We might think that Catherine's flirtatious
behaviour was understandable, if unwise, but
in Tudor times, following the Act of Treason
in 1534, it was suicidal.

Catherine Parr

HENRY WAITED OVER A YEAR before deciding to marry again and his choice this time was very different. Catherine Parr did not represent a political alliance, she was not young and, happily for her, she was not expected to bear the king children. Catherine was born in 1512, the eldest child of Sir Thomas Parr of Kendal, who had risen to be controller of the Royal Household. After Catherine's first husband died in 1532, she married Lord Latimer. When he became an invalid, the couple moved to London where he could get better treatment. Here Catherine became friendly with Princess Mary and, increasingly, with Thomas Seymour, one of Jane Seymour's brothers.

In 1543 the king, who was looking for a companion for his old age, alighted on Catherine, and, even before Latimer died on 2 March 1543, he started to send her presents. When the king asked Catherine to marry him, she was torn between love for Thomas Seymour and duty to the king. Duty won, and on 12 July the marriage took place.

Being childless, she cared for Elizabeth and Edward, who were just ten and six years old, as though they were her own children. She calmed Henry down when he raged, comforted him when he was depressed, and sat with his painful, ulcerated leg on her lap.

By Christmas 1546, Henry was dying, but he sent Catherine and his court to Greenwich while he remained in London. He died on 28 January 1547. Catherine must have been relieved at Henry's death and in June she married Thomas Seymour, her fourth husband. She was very happy but the marriage was short. She became pregnant and gave birth to a daughter in August 1548, but, like Jane Seymour before her, she died shortly afterwards of childbed fever.

CATHERINE PARR
Catherine Parr was lively, friendly and kind. Only Anne of Cleves objected to her marriage to Henry. Anne declared, probably correctly, that Catherine was less beautiful than herself.

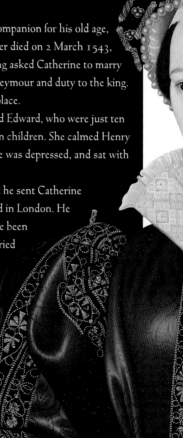

CATHERINE PARR'S BADGE
Catherine Parr's badge shows a crowned maiden rising from a Tudor rose. Her motto was 'To be useful in all I do'.

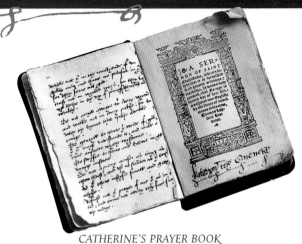

CATHERINE'S PRAYER BOOK

This prayer book dated 1534 contains Catherine's handwriting. She was an ardent Protestant and later wrote a prayer book of her own.

A CLOSE SHAVE

Although Henry had separated from the church of Rome, he was no Lutheran Protestant. Catherine often talked to Henry about religion, however, and was accused of pushing her Protestant views too strongly. It looked as if Catherine too might end up in the Tower of London, but she claimed that she had talked to the king only to learn from him. Catherine was saved. This Victorian painting by William Hamilton shows Henry reproving Sir Thomas Wriothesley for attempting to arrest the queen.

CATHERINE'S TOMB

Catherine's tomb can be seen in the Chapel of Sudeley Castle.

SUDELEY CASTLE

Catherine came to Sudeley in June 1548 to give birth to her child. She died here in September 1548, six days after the birth.

The Heirs

ALTHOUGH PRINCE EDWARD WAS ONLY NINE when Henry died, Henry was content that he had provided England with a king to follow him. Edward VI's reign was short-lived, however, and all three of Henry's legitimate children reigned.

Henry left a nation divided into Catholics and Protestants, a division that dominated the reigns of all his children. When Edward, a Protestant, died of tuberculosis in 1553, he was, despite plots to prevent it, eventually succeeded by Mary. Having endured religious persecution herself she did not hesitate to inflict it on others in her determination to make England Catholic again. In 1554 Mary married Philip, son of the king of Spain.

She was then 38 years old, but to prevent the country falling into the Protestant hands of her sister Elizabeth, Mary, like Henry, was desperate for the birth of an heir. She even thought that she was pregnant twice, but each time her hopes proved false. Philip was not enamoured of his wife and spent most of his time out of the country, leaving Mary to die alone in 1558.

Philip did not dispute Elizabeth's succession to the English throne, assuming that he would now marry her and so retain his power. Elizabeth, however, did not marry Philip, and, in spite of pleas from her ministers, did not marry anyone. She frequently entered diplomatic negotiations for marriage but always added impossible conditions at the last moment. People said she enjoyed power too much to share it, but it seemed at times that she genuinely tried to marry but could not bring herself to do so. Perhaps the traumas of her childhood were too great for her to overcome. So none of Henry's heirs produced an heir, and at Elizabeth's death in 1603 the Tudors' crown passed to the Scottish king, James Stuart.

QUEEN ELIZABETH

Elizabeth was a popular queen who said of herself that although she was a woman she had 'the heart and stomach of a king'. During her long reign of 45 years England became powerful and prosperous.

ROSARY
Henry's royal arms are carved into the Pater bead showing that this rosary was most probably his.